A Personal Journey to
good health and

WHAT ARE YOU WAITING FOR?

Today's the Best Day to Start "Living"

by

Paula Lesso

outskirts
press

TABLE OF CONTENTS

PREFACE

....

This book was created to have a conversation with you and for you to have one with yourself. Look at your Present, your Future, your Mindset and, most importantly, your Self Talk and how it increases or decreases your growth.

My goal is to share my Personal Journey and the paths I took for me to now live the life I love. I am proud to add writing this book to other achievements - life coach, corporate trainer, mentor, motivational speaker, triathlete, CrossFit athlete, runner, health and fitness advocate, and ballroom dancer.

This book is about will I, do I want to, should I and how about? I want this information to jumpstart your creative juices and push deeper thinking about your personal and professional journey to help you move forward mentally, physically and emotionally. The time to "Awaken Your Brilliance" is now.

This is your call to action!

Take time to journal your thoughts; write about the things that speak to you. Celebrate special moments. Dump negative thoughts, actions and people.

Use the blank pages at the end of each chapter to capture goals and plans, special moments, achievements and celebrations, large and small. If you need to write more, you can use a journal, a notebook, 3x5 cards or a steno book - whatever resonates with you.

ACKNOWLEDGEMENTS

"Congratulations, Paula on this courageous self-exploration and sharing of private thoughts with all of us. What a journey you have been on! I am thankful to have been with you for some of your experiences."

> *Patty Decker*, Business Services Manager, Corning, NY

"What Are You Waiting For? is an enjoyable read with practical tools and exercises that will challenge you to become a better version of yourself starting today!"

> *Ty Burton*, Author, A Journey to Manhood, Charlotte, NC

"Paula Lesso knows what she writes not only because of her professional training but mostly because of the courage she has used to meet challenges in her own life. This is the kind of little book you keep on the night stand or in your pocketbook **_or briefcase_** to reread periodically as a reminder of the power you possess in creating your own life."

> *Patrice Gaines*, Author, Laughing in the Dark, Lake Wylie, SC

"This book is excellent and honestly was right on time for me! I truly enjoyed the book and admire your bravery in sharing your life experiences to motivate others. *What Are You Waiting For?* provides a new and refreshing approach to motivating readers through real life experiences that will literally propel you to take control of your life and realize your dreams."

Miesha Burton, Operational Risk
Management Professional, Charlotte, NC

"I love this book. I got a sneak peak just at the right time in my life. I've been on an emotional roller coaster for about a year. I had gotten away from a lot of the principles that you referenced in the book. This book was just what I needed to put me back into focus. It helped me realize that I (not situations) had been getting in my own way. What am I waiting for? Thanks again for this book. It will bless a lot of people."

Nicholas Riggins, Managing Principal,
HOH Consulting Firm, Air Force veteran,
and college veterans services director,
Charlotte, NC

FROM THE AUTHOR

This page was the hardest to write. So many people to thank and acknowledge. I thank those who said the picture on the back of my business card is a book cover. That comment led me to consider writing a book about my journey from Corning, NY to Charlotte, NC, Looking at that picture helped me decide on the title.

Thank you to those I told I was writing a book, what it was about and them saying, "let me know when it is available and I will buy it!" That pushed me to get it completed.

My dad, Joe; sister, Kathy-Jo and brother, Michael. They supported and cheered me on during this huge undertaking.

All my friends that anxiously awaited while I wrote and would ask, "how is it going?"

All the prayers that were said.

And to Glenn Proctor, my business partner who gave me deadlines to keep me motivated. He pushed, prodded, and provided writing tips. His edits and suggestions helped stretch me to write when I didn't want to and to show vulnerability. He was right. The process has been fun, frustrating and amazing all at the same time. It has opened me up to new ways of expressing myself. His excitement for me receiving my first published copy spurred me on, increasing my anticipation of forever being known as an author.

THE QUESTIONS

What are you waiting for?
Waiting to be happy before moving forward?
Waiting to lose weight before going to the gym?
Waiting to get the right job before you feel accomplished?
Waiting to quit your job and start your business?
Waiting for the exact opportunity to wear that new outfit?
Waiting to date?
Waiting to call him or her to ask them out?
Waiting to call him or her to get a cup of coffee?
Waiting for the perfect relationship?
Waiting to end a bad relationship?
Waiting to have a baby before feeling like a family?
Waiting for someone else to apologize first?
Waiting for procrastination to go away?
Waiting to take your dream vacation?
Waiting to finish your degree or get back in school?
Waiting to write a book?
Waiting to call for a doctor's appointment?
Waiting because of fear?
Waiting for your Fairy God Mother?
Waiting for your Prince Charming?
Waiting for _____?

I have the question, ***What Am I Waiting For?*** on the white board in my office. I look at it everyday. Those five words help me to focus on priorities. It's so easy to put things off until tomorrow, next week, next month or next year. Or forever…

I saw a sign that reads: "There are 7 days in a Week, Someday is Not One of Them!"

It's time to get moving and stop putting things off. Do it now!

When I would say to my mom, I am waiting, she would say, "Weight (wait) broke the wagon." It took me a long time to understand what it meant.

Take a Moment:

As you continue your Personal Journey, own whatever it is you are waiting for. Say the below sentences out loud, emphasize the word that is bolded. Choose which one feels right. Then consider, meditate or journal why you chose that one.

What am I waiting for?
What ***Am*** I waiting for?
What am ***I*** waiting for?
What am I ***Waiting*** for?
What am I waiting ***For***?

Throughout the book, if there are areas you relate to, change you to "I" and reread it. This creates a sense of ownership. I want you to feel that.

ARE YOU
SEEING STRAIGHT?

Clarity

Get the Glass Cleaner

Does your present or future seem foggy? Is there a film on your mirror when you see your face? Are you letting life happen, rather than making life happen?

(This is an example of where you can use I. "I let, or I allow, life to happen, rather than I make life happen").

What does that look like? How does that feel?

Get **Clarity** in your life. Get the glass cleaner and clean your mirror, get rid of the cobwebs and clutter. I want you to see you clearly! I want you to love that person in the mirror. I want you to say to that gorgeous face, "I love you, I am happy." "I am awesome." (I said those words while going through my divorce).

When my husband left, I had a conversation with my dad and told him that my husband and I were separating. His question to me, "Paula Jean, what do you want?" My reply, "I just want to be happy." I was able to say that without hesitation. I had clarity.

After working with my counselor, and journaling for months, I looked in the mirror one day, and said out loud, "I am happy!"

I had lunch with my dad the next week, and reminded him

of our conversation and the question he asked me. I looked him in the eyes, and said, "I am happy". He was thrilled.

Clarity brings Confidence. Have a clear idea of your goals and plans. Be specific.

I was clear and confident that I wanted to get married and be a stay-at-home mom. I was not a career person. After I got married, my husband and I decided that I would work until I got pregnant.

It took two years of trying before we went to an infertility doctor. We went through testing and I was on infertility drugs for a year. No results. One option was to adopt, but my husband was not on board for that. I had to accept that we were not going to have kids.

I wish I could have given my parents' grandchildren. It took decades for me to let that go. I was able to let it go in my mid 50s after talking with a body whisperer, an alternative medicine practitioner who helps people understand how their physical symptoms frequently contain messages from their spirits.

As much as I wanted be an awesome mother and have grandchildren for my parents, they understood it was ok.

I had a friend who was also trying to start a family and the woman was so intent on getting pregnant that she had difficulty being around pregnant women. She did not want to hear about other women getting pregnant.

For me, God had another plan. He did. I had a great corporate career and now as a life coach, I am doing what lights me up – guiding others to live healthier lives, set personal and professional goals, find meaningful relationships and determine new levels of success.

Take A Moment:

Get clarity on what you want:

- start working out, or change your routine: decide where, when and how many days
- a new (newer) car: choose type, exterior and interior color, options
- a new job: what company or same, maybe in a different department, people you want to work with
- a new home: decide how big, how many rooms, location
- a new relationship or improve the one you have: how do you want it to be different?

This is where a vision board can make a difference. Attend my visioning workshop. In these sessions, attendees identify in specific detail through words and pictures on poster boards their "future" or goals. It can be pictures of money, houses, vacations, cars, fitness and weight goals, career titles or words that inspire you. With your poster, you have a visual representation of the life you want. View it every day.

What am I waiting for?

Clutter & Clarity

Clutter. Does it affect your growth, happiness and mental health?

Yes. Clutter in your mind, in your space (home, office, garage, phones, laptops) is slowing you down. We don't realize how much stress clutter causes until we're out from under it!

Limit distractions. Clean your personal and professional space. Take inventory of your social media. Take a hard look at those (family, friends and colleagues) around you. It's easier to live in a streamlined environment than in a jumbled one. Or else your clutter will haunt you three, six or nine months or a year later.

I believe one area out of sync can and will affect other areas in your life. For example, home affects work and work affects home. It's time to clear the clutter. Where do you start?

Start small. That can be in increments of time or area(s) you want to work on. Make a list.

Let's say you are cleaning out a closet or a pantry. How much time do you want to devote to this task? If it is 30 minutes, set a timer for 30 minutes, and when the timer sounds, stop. You can reassess if you are making progress and if you're not ready to stop, set the timer for another 30 minutes.

One thing that works for me is to get help. A friend came over and assisted me in organizing and decluttering my office. I set time aside and allowed no distractions. As we worked, we caught up on what was happening in our lives.

Because we got so much accomplished, I now enjoy walking into my office. Rather than running in, finding what I needed, and running back out, I spend time in my office!

Taking action eliminates clutter. Inaction is procrastination. Yes, I just said the "p" word!

Remember, you can fall victim to old ways of thinking and fall back into old habits at anytime. Positive thinking – sometimes, with the help of a good coach – brings positive action and eliminates procrastination and clutter.

I know. I have to work on lessening old habits. My recovery time is faster as I put my positive mindset in place. Is there a reminder you could find to lessen the possibility of this happening?

My paperweight that says "I Got This" immediately raises my confidence level. I also have a picture of a frog on my bulletin board, with his head tilted (how a dog tilts his head when he is not sure what he has heard or seen). Every time, I look at the frog, I think he is saying, "Really?" I then ask myself, " Is this the most productive thing I could be doing right now?"

What motivates you? Is it a saying, a picture, a photograph, a drawing, a medal, a trophy, positive acknowledgements from others or personal affirmations? What's your affirmation?

Think about these popular quotes.

"Insanity: doing the same thing over and over again and expecting different results." Albert Einstein

"We are what we repeatedly do. Therefore, excellence is not an act, but a habit." Aristotle

Now that you have started to de-clutter, define what you really **Want**. In defining your want, confidence grows because you are getting clearer about the Want. Define it in great detail.

What color is it? What size is it? Is it a new job, business or relationship?

What lights you up? I want you to write about it. Write down everything - no matter how far-fetched it may seem. Is it singing, being a chef, a painter, an entrepreneur? Turn the editor off in your head that says, "No, I can't do that." "I'll never be able to have that." Yes you can! It is visioning (visual or written) the **Want** that will produce the action of achieving success.

Identifying *'by when'* gets you even closer. Put a date on it;

make it real. Have daily, weekly, monthly and yearly goals. It can push you. It does me. Yet, sometimes, I hope my accountability partners, and mentors won't ask me *by when*. I'm happy when they do. I use *by when* with my coaching clients. They find it helpful to have a target to work towards. Get clear about who you are.

Motivation is a key to getting what you want. Another key is having an accountability partner. Jessica Adkins, my friend at CrossFit, is my workout partner. We meet a minimum of three times a week; knowing that not being there will disappoint the other. She motivates me to get my butt to the workout. I have to keep my word.

"Integrity, doing what I say I am going to do, when I say I am going to do it. Integrity is honoring your word, even to yourself. Nothing works without integrity."

Here is a saying posted on my fridge:

"Self-discipline is the ability to make yourself do what you should do, when you should do it, whether you feel like it or not." Elbert Hubbard

My re-write:

"Self-discipline is the ability to make myself do what I should do, when I should do it, whether I feel like it or not. Self-discipline is key to personal greatness."

Seeing this on the fridge, especially when I don't feel like doing something, pushes me to do the thing right then rather than waiting until later when it may not be as convenient. Have you ever wished the next morning you had prepared your lunch or your clothes the night before because in the morning things didn't go quite as you had planned and now you are rushing?

We don't live life all at once. Some things take baby steps.

What am I waiting for?

A Story to Live By

by Ann Wells (Los Angeles Times)

This story was forwarded to me by e-mail

My brother-in-law opened the bottom drawer of my sister's bureau and lifted out a tissue-wrapped package. "This," he said, "is not a slip. This is lingerie." He discarded the tissue and handed me the slip. It was exquisite; silk, handmade and trimmed with a cobweb of lace. The price tag with an astronomical figure on it was still attached. "Jan bought this the first time we went to New York, at least 8 or 9 years ago. She never wore it. She was saving it for a special occasion. Well, I guess this is the occasion." He took the slip from me and put it on the bed with the other clothes we were taking to the mortician. His hands lingered on the soft material for a moment, then he slammed the drawer shut and turned to me. "Don't ever save anything for a special occasion. Every day you're alive is a special occasion."

I remembered those words through the funeral and the days that followed when I helped him and my niece attend to all the sad chores that follow an unexpected death. I thought about them on the plane returning to California from the Midwestern town where my sister's family lives. I thought about all the things that she hadn't seen or heard or done. I thought about the things that she had done without realizing that they were special. I'm still thinking about his words, and they've changed my life.

I'm reading more and dusting less. I'm sitting on the deck and admiring the view without fussing about the weeds in the garden. I'm spending more time with my family and friends and less time in committee meetings. Whenever possible, life should be a pattern of experience to savor, not endure. I'm trying to recognize these moments now and cherish them.

I'm not "saving" anything; we use our good china and crystal for every special event-such as losing a pound, getting the sink unstopped, the first camellia blossom.

I wear my good blazer to the market if I feel like it. My theory is if I look prosperous, I can shell out $28.49 for one small bag of groceries without wincing. I'm not saving my good perfume for special parties; clerks in hardware stores and tellers in banks have noses that function as well as my party-going friends'.

"Someday" and "one of these days" are losing their grip on my vocabulary. If it's worth seeing or hearing or doing, I want to see and hear and do it now. I'm not sure what my sister would have done had she known that she wouldn't be here for the tomorrow we all take for granted. I think she would have called family members and a few close friends. She might have called a few former friends to apologize and mend fences for past squabbles. I like to think she would have gone out for a Chinese dinner, her favorite food. I'm guessing-I'll never know.

It's those little things left undone that would make me angry if I knew that my hours were limited. Angry because I put off seeing good friends whom I was going to get in touch with --- someday. Angry because I hadn't written certain letters that I intended to write --- one of these days. Angry and sorry that I didn't tell my husband and daughter often enough how much I truly love them.

I'm trying very hard not to put off, hold back, or save anything that would add laughter and luster to our lives. And, every morning when I open my eyes, I tell myself that it is special. Every day, every minute, every breath truly is...a gift from God.

Like the above "A Story to Live By" says, don't wait.

"When you arise in the morning, think of waht a precious privilege it is to be alive - to **breathe**, to **think**, to **enjoy**, to **love**." Marcus Aurelius

I remember when my mom would motice I wanted to wear something I just bought, and say, "Save that for a special occasion." I would wear it anyway, either out of spite or what I wanted to wear. Of course there were times when I would spill something on the outfit and think, if I had only waited. When my mom died, my sister and I went through her closet. There were clothes with tags on them that she never wore. My sister and I are able to wear some of them and others we donated.

What occasion are you waiting for to wear that new outfit or piece of clothing?

"Wear it, use it or donate it."

What *am* I waiting for?

Change & Challenges

We all have experienced change. Look back at the changes that have happened in your life, from the very first time you can remember until today. What do they mean? Recognize those changes – many that have happened and those you made happen.

I realized the changes I've experienced in my life - school, friends, college, marriage, divorce, infertility, moving without a job, job change, death of a parent, break ups and relationships.

What came from those challenges is change. I challenged myself to live beyond divorce. I was 43 at the time. I am 60 at the time of this writing and I have lived a lot in those 17 years!

I could have curled up in a corner and never moved forward. I have seen and heard of so many people that allow that to happen. I had a couple of pity parties, when I would cry and ask, "why me?" After each of my pity parties I became stronger. This change was a gift of rebirth and renewal.

What are you allowing to happen in your life?

Are you allowing work to take over your life? Is there a promotion or job you have your eye on and not going for it? Are you giving your power over to your boss, or company? Have you asked for an increase, sought a promotion or questioned the increase you received when your review reflected superior work?

Are you allowing someone, including a partner or spouse to sabotage your dreams? Is fear holding you back? Look in the mirror and say out loud: "*Fear*, you will not hold me back."

Take a moment to reflect on these questions:

1. Am I keeping myself small? Do I promote myself? Do I ask for what I want?

I realized I was keeping myself small in my life coaching business. When it came to marketing, branding or promoting, I had limited experience and found those who could help. I took the challenge to brand and promote myself better.

Now, it's easy for me to tell prospects what I do, how I can help them and why they want to work with me. My corporate colleagues and friends often asked me, "If you don't promote you, who will?" Have you heard that before?

I stepped out. I have a team – a coaching business partner, and two professional women who handle social media and administration. This happened through effective networking.

No matter how small, or loud your voice may be, ask for help. Even in the Wizard of Oz, the Tin Man asked for help. If the Tin Man didn't ask for help, he would still be stuck!

2. Have you allowed someone in your life to hold you back?

I have. The person I moved to Charlotte with in 2003 held me back financially. I paid all the bills and he kept promising to contribute his half. We were together for five years before I ended the relationship.

He still owes me money. I allowed that to happen. After several attempts to collect the money, I let it go. Lesson learned.

This part of my life happened because, like most relationships, it was fresh and new.

We met when I took golf lessons from him during the spring of 2003.

Weeks later, I took a break to visit my best friend, Mary, in Memphis, TN. When I returned, I called the golf pro to make up my missed lessons. It ended up being just the golf pro and me for the last two lessons. During those lessons, I found out he had lived near my paternal grandparents and his father was a teacher at my high school. I mentioned I was moving south. After I finished the lessons, we started dating.

In the first part of this chapter, I mentioned the word clarity. Clarity is focus. Clarity is defining what you want and choosing what you are going to work on.

If there is someone working in an industry that you are interested in, ask to meet for coffee. Share your ideas (not all of your plan) and ask for their input. The key questions: How did you reach your level of success? What steps do you recommend I take? Who else do you suggest I speak with? Are there any books you recommend I read?

Remember, performance is made up of action and inaction. You are either in action or inaction. It depends on your goal and when you want to complete it. Decide your *by when*.

Do you have a bucket list? I didn't have a bucket list and realized that if I didn't make a list, I would not focus on what's left to achieve. I now have a bucket list. Because of changes in my life, my list includes goals and challenges I never thought about.

Even before making my list, I finished a number of fitness competitions because I was challenged to try. A number of friends pushed me to become more fit. As a result, I am stronger and healthier than I have ever been.

I realize now I am very competitive. I am always looking for the next physical challenge. I've competed in fitness challenges every year in Charlotte since 2013. Before that, I do not remember being competitive or competing.

It's because of the classes at CrossFit Steele Creek that brought out my competitiveness.

First, I have to want to compete. It takes determination, training, commitment, risk in trying something new, structure, accountability and positive self-talk.

- I completed a Warrior Dash in 2013 (*with my friend, Anna Maria, from CrossFit. This was the first time I ran through mud, water and fire.*)
- Ran Ortho Carolina 10k and the Thunder Road half marathon both in 2014. (*I challenged myself to see if I could run a 10k and the half followed. I celebrated with the largest Reese's cup sundae I could get. I enjoyed EVERY bite!*)
- Became a life coach in 2008 and started my life coaching business in January 2014.
- Competed in ballroom dancing in 2015 at Planet Ballroom. I won first place in the Rumba. (*The competition fell on what would have been on my mom's 90th birthday. I always loved watching my parents glide on the dance floor. All this from when I won lessons and fell in love with it*)
- Completed the Ramblin' Rose triathlon in 2016. I trained with Tri it for Life and now I am a triathlete and was a mentor for the 2017 event. (*My running friend Lee asked me to do the triathlon*).
- Decided to write this book in 2016 (*My business partner Glenn Proctor challenged me*).

I look forward to new personal and professional challenges. What is my next thing going to be? To help me stay focused, I put my challenges on my vision board at the beginning of each year.

Celebrate EVERY Milestone!

In 2016, I spoke about the competitive events and accomplishments at a "Map Your Way to Health Seminar" for Every Woman Can Be, a woman's empowerment group. I presented "One Body, One You". As I mentioned each competition and put on the medals I earned, the women were amazed that I continue to compete at this level at age 60.

"There is no reason for this body to slow down. I feel great!"

This is what I say to anyone seeking better health: "Do what feels right for you. For me, my lifelong goal is to stay fit and to help others stay healthy."

Have you had a friend challenge you to do something positive and you said, "No"?

Do you want to volunteer for something and don't?

Do you need to know the outcome of a challenge before you take it on?

I used to be like that. I froze. I didn't want to look stupid if I did something wrong. Afterwards, I wish I had participated.

I was in a training class and the facilitators were looking for volunteers to introduce skits and speakers the next morning. I wasn't sure what was expected, so I didn't volunteer. I wanted to do it right.

The next morning after the introductions and skits were completed, I realized I could have handled it easily. The facilitators would have made sure I knew what was expected. I was waiting to see what it looked like first! A lost opportunity.

Try something new. Start small. Is there a skill you want to learn, a class you want to take, do motivational speaking, write a book, or learn gardening?

Experience life! Jump in!

I didn't know what a book was supposed to look like. Glenn Proctor, my editor and business partner, told me to start writing. I did. I knew he would help me be successful. Who is the person you can rely on?

Take A Moment:

Challenge yourself.
Step out.
Take a risk.

I challenge You to *Be A Better Version of Yourself*

We are who we are. Is there something you would like to improve? Take on?
Stretch out of your comfort zone.
Be You, Everyone else is taken!

What am *I* waiting for?

OPPORTUNITY

*Another Layer
(What, Where, When,
Why, How, Own It)*

Relationships

I went through a divorce in Corning after being married 21 years. I never wanted the "d" word as part of my vocabulary.

I had to face the fact that my husband was having an affair. I was not going to be a marriage of one. It hurt: no getting around it. I couldn't believe it was happening to me!

Divorce hurts families and friends. My brother lived in the next town and I would go over at different times to talk to him. He would let me cry and vent. My friend, Mary, had been through a divorce (happily married now). I went to her house and she gave me tissues as I cried. Patty, another friend who is divorced, and I met weekly to laugh and have serious conversations.

Family and friends helped me heal. However, the most important person for me at that time was Peg, my wellness counselor. I had been seeing her prior to the affair because after 17 years, I wanted to get the passion back into my marriage. I thought it was up to me to figure it out. During the counseling, she and I agreed I was grieving the decline of my marriage.

I didn't tell my husband I was seeing a counselor (he traveled frequently for work, so I would see her when he was gone). I was certain that if I told him I was seeing a counselor, he would ask me how much it cost.

I paid out-of-pocket for two reasons: 1. I was worth it. 2. My survival was at stake.

After nearly a year, Peg recommended we see a marriage counselor. We visited a male marriage counselor twice before splitting. During the first session, I found out my husband thought we were going separate ways. Before the second session I found evidence he was seeing someone else. I assume his being unhappy was the reason for the affair.

It doesn't hurt anymore. The divorce was a gift. I would never have moved from upstate New York to Charlotte and become a life coach.

If you are unhappy in your marriage or relationship, work on it before having an affair. What caused you to fall in love with your partner or spouse in the first place? Have you let things go: your health, your desires or your communication? Did you find in that new person what is missing in your relationship?

If you decide to speak with a counselor, find out what is missing. If you are able to work things out and stay together, great. If not, leaving the relationship may be the best option.

Think about this: A separation, divorce or an affair can have an effect on family and friends for years.

It took two years to finalize the divorce. Seeing a counselor was the best thing for me. It helped me understand what my contribution was to the relationship, how to heal and in the process, I was able to help others that were affected. Because I took care of myself, physically and mentally, it helped my family and friends see how strong I was.

Years after the divorce, I was in a passive/aggressive relationship. I knew two months into the relationship I should have left. It is hard to leave even when red flags pop up. I found out what being in a passive/aggressive relationship is about. It is tiring and negative. I knew something wasn't right and couldn't identify it until I was out from under it.

He was loving and supportive at times, and other times telling me, "You don't know how to find a job, you don't need to network, you don't have a heart."

Listen to friends or acquaintances when they say you shouldn't be treated like that. I had to step back and take inventory to realize this relationship was not in my best interest. I was giving, but not receiving, the love and support a relationship should be built on.

Toward the end of the relationship, when he would get angry, he threw things. That was scary. At the time, I didn't want to be alone and held on to the passive attention. Eighteen months after it started, I ended it.

Funny how he didn't get his passive/aggressive destructive behavior affected the relationship. Yelling was common growing up in his household. It was not common in mine and I was not going to be around it.

This is why anyone with relationship issues, should get professional help, individually or as a couple. So much of what is missing is communication. I look back at my marriage and relationships and see that effective communication was lacking. We had gotten comfortable.

I have seen people lose hope when life-changing events such as divorce, job loss, death of a pet, a friend or family member occur. It's time to get professional help, a third party objective person or team to help you understand situations more clearly.

Family & friends are great for support, but be careful. They have biased opinions and are not professionals.

I became a life coach to help clients and others move barriers. Often, a person must realize a family member, work or personal situation is holding them back. Or, they have to get out of their own head.

What are you waiting for in your relationship? Is it new? Do you need to set boundaries? Have you been in it for a while - six months, a year, five, 10, 20 years or more and has it gotten comfortable?

How would you define your current relationship? If you are not happy, more than likely, your significant other isn't either. If there is no sharing or support, there is no relationship. Remember what brought you together and is that feeling or reason still there? If you can't have the deep meaningful conversations, the relationship is in trouble. Is it time to move on?

I will not settle for anyone who doesn't have similar interests. Someone athletic, a sports enthusiast, spiritual, can go from jeans to suit, enjoys concerts, Broadway plays, enjoys dancing, adventurous, great listener and communicator, likes to travel, likes to cook, try new foods, and person to laugh and cry with. Two of the most important things: a man with manners and a sense of humor.

Who are you looking for? Do you truly know? Be honest with yourself. Do you have it written down? Be specific.

"Communication is the heart of any relationship." - Paula Lesso

What am I *waiting* for?

How Well Do You Know Your Mom, Your Dad?

My mom passed away in 2014 at age 89. I wish I had spent more time with her and found out what it was like to be the next to the youngest of 10 children. How was it being raised by her dad and her older sisters? (her mom died when she was seven). What does she remember about her mom? How did she learn to knit argyle socks? (She taught me how to knit). Why did she and my fraternal grandmother not get along? What happened to cause that? I asked my dad: he wasn't sure. I asked my sister and brother and they didn't know.

I learned some things about my mom from my dad. How they met, what her dad was like, how it was hanging out with her siblings, how they used to go dancing and bowling. The fun they had. Raising three kids.

Last time I was home in Corning, I sat with my dad to learn more about him. The oldest of two boys; they grew up in Corning. He talked about he and his brother, two years younger, loved to sit in front of the ironing board to listen to their mother sing. He told stories about his World War II Air Force experience and his time at the Corning Glass Works factory. He then had an executive career in banking. Now retired, he is selling real estate at age 91.

I am blessed to have this time with him. He is documenting his life, so my siblings and I have that history to appreciate.

Have you thought about what your parents experienced, individually and together, before you came along? Ask them as soon as you can. It will give you insight to their upbringing and yours. What struggles did they experience and overcome? What were their goals?

What am I *waiting* for?

Messages

What message are you waiting for? Is someone telling you what you should do? If so, you are giving them your power. Take 100 percent responsibility for your actions.

In November 2002, I was caught in the downturn of Corning, Inc. and knew it was time for a change. It was about three years after the divorce.

Later that month, while attending the local high school rivalry football game, I received a clear message. As I scanned the Corning horizon, a voice said, "I will not be here in a year." Hearing that was life-changing. And then, I heard it again. "I will not be here in a year." I had a *by when*.

During the next year, I repeated to family and friends that I was moving to Charlotte. I had been to Charlotte several times and loved the energy and beauty of the area. My destination was chosen. In November 2003, it happened.

As summer turned to fall, it was getting closer to the one-year moving deadline. I was tired of hearing myself say, "I was moving" without taking action. I asked the golf pro to selfishly move with me (he was divorced with two young sons). If he said no, I had to end the relationship. If he said yes, then we'd be together. He said yes. We moved to Charlotte on November 3, 2003, nearly one year to the date of my message.

I signed up with a temporary agency to find work. I got a position as an administrative assistant at a bank to get my foot in the door. Nine months later, I was hired permanently. My goal was to get into the training area of the Corporate and Investment Banking division. I became the project coordinator in training and development.

The voice that prompted my move to Charlotte was the second time I received such a clear message.

The first was the morning of my divorce deposition. I was lying in bed and asked God, "What do I need to know?" The message was strong and clear. "Today is my day." It repeated, "today is my day." The deposition went well.

It's wonderful to get clear messages about important life decisions. I still ask, "what do I need to know?" and listen.

The key is being open to messages of opportunity.

Where do you look for opportunities? Where do your opportunities for work, entrepreneurial pursuits, or personal relationships come from? Are you seeing the signs and making the effort to find your best opportunities?

I tell my clients and friends they will know - call it gut feel, intuition or a sign - when it is time to take action.

One phrase I learned during my coaching training was the

use of *next appropriate action*, that feeling when you want to immediately take action on the thing you are thinking about.

What physical, mental, emotional and spiritual messages are you receiving? Identify what they mean and how they can help you create the life you want.

How creative are you in visualizing your future? Having a vision board is a great place to start and can be created at any time. It's simple: get construction paper or poster board, and tear out pictures and words from magazines that represent what you want. Some possibilities: travel, house, financial stability, peace, relationships, better job, exercise – or anything that you want for your life. It can be of things you want now or in the future.

Post your vision board where you see it everyday. You can create the vision on your computer, print it off and carry it with you. Another technique is to put your vision on 3x5 cards and post them on your refrigerator and mirrors. Adding a *by when* promotes accountability.

Take A Moment:

What do you want to achieve or accomplish in the next year?
What are your goals?
What do you want to focus on?
Which goal is the most important?
Why do you want it?
When do you want it?

When I do visioning workshops, the goal is to guide participants to realize the important things in their lives and create the extraordinary life they envision.

What am I *waiting* for?

Touch

Touch. It can heal us all.

One Sunday at Forest Hill Church in Charlotte, Senior Pastor David Chadwick had the congregation stand and hold hands, (this was in 2016 during a time of civil unrest in Charlotte). He spoke about how great it was to see black and white parishioners "holding hands in harmony. This might be the only touch some people will have all week." His statement brought me to tears. As I walked back to my car, I started creating my poem about Touch.

I told a friend why I wrote about Touch. She said I needed to include it in the book. It touched her emotionally. My heart aches as it did that day, thinking that touch is not part of everyone's daily life.

Touch

What is touch?
Touch is soft
As a cloud
Touch is hard as wood

Touch can be warm and welcoming
Touch can be cold and rejecting

A loving touch, soft gentle kisses
Passionate deep kisses

Touch of lips on lips
On the back of your neck on your forehead

Touch of gentle love taps
Touch of hands holding
Hugs embracing

Eyes locking touch souls
Speaking volumes with out words

Touch can be a slap
Regrets
Withdrawing
Hurting
Cowering

Touch can be
Exhilarating
Passionate
Loving
Caring
Rejuvenating
Awakening

Now, later
Too long between touches
Touching all the time
Touching self
Touching others

What is your touch?
How do you like to be touched?
When and where?

Cuddling touches
Frigid touches
Scary touches
Soft touches

Touch of cool sheets
On a hot summer night
Touch of fleece sheets
On a cold winter night

Fabrics touch, silkiness, wool,
Linen, cotton

Touch all 5 senses
Hearing of laughter, the best medicine
Sounds of warning or music touching the soul
Tears of sadness or happiness
Smell to pique our appetite
Taste of salty tears or food
Sour or sweet
Seeing the beauty of us, connecting to nature
So much to touch

Words touch of regret or love
Touch of two souls

Here and Beyond
Human and Animal

Touch

What am I waiting *for*?

Body, Health and Mindset

What are you waiting for when it comes to your body, health and mindset? What does being healthy mean to you? In the beginning of the book, I posed this question: Are you waiting to lose weight before going to the gym? Going to CrossFit is my way to stay in shape, maintain weight and be part of a motivational community.

How does your body shape or image affect how you feel about your health? If you say you are too fat, out of shape and unworthy, and believe there is nothing you can do about it, you're wrong. There is always something we can do to improve our physical and mental health.

Get a positive mindset! Think about your body! Reach out to someone who is in the shape you want to be in and ask questions. Every health and exercise regimen has a beginning. Start slow. The will to continue resides with you. Others have done it. You can do it too!

If I don't work out and eat healthy, I will gain weight. I am five-foot-four and weigh 123 pounds. To maintain my weight, I go to CrossFit three times a week, run 2-3 miles twice a week and walk six miles twice a week. I eat protein, vegetables and fruit. I love food as my family and friends will attest.

And, I like sweets! Still, I don't deny myself. I use my

WWHM method - when, what and how much. I enjoy every bite!

In 1998, while going through challenges in my marriage, I gained weight. I had no will power to stop eating. I remember standing in my kitchen in Corning, feeling the tightness of my pants and thinking, "I have many clothes in my closet I enjoy wearing and I am NOT going to replace them with a larger size." That was my trigger to eat less and lose weight. I wanted to maintain the body shape and weight I had as an active teenager.

When I worked at Corning, they had Weight Watchers during the lunch hour. If I attended 80 percent of the meetings and lost a minimum of five pounds – what I needed to lose - I would be reimbursed for the 16-week session. I took the challenge. I learned to drink more water, eat more fruit, stop eating food I didn't like and stop eating when I felt full. I weighed 128 - my heaviest ever.

It took the full 16 weeks to lose the five pounds! I would go down a pound one week, and up a half pound the next.

I achieved my goal at the final weigh in of the last week of the session. I've been a lifetime member for nearly 20 years. Part of being a life member is a monthly Weight Watchers weigh in. I've maintained 123 pounds for almost two decades.

You can change your eating habits. You can purchase and

prepare healthy food. You can find time for better health. As my business partner says, "eat right, exercise and get sleep." We can help.

Are you on medication(s)? What if you were able to get rid of the pills or reduce the number you take?

What is the trigger that will make a difference in your health? Don't blame your family, a relationship, or a childhood memory. Even if you have a life threatening disease, seek information or ask a medical or health professional how you can improve your health. Take charge of you!

Take a Moment:

(1) Make health a priority.
(2) Schedule exercise. Start slow (check with a doctor before starting a routine).
(3) Learn healthy eating habits.
(4) Find an accountability partner
(5) Get naysayers out of your way

What steps are you going to take today to achieve better health? Be honest with yourself. *By when* are you going to take action?

Starting an exercise routine is tough. Begin with a 10-minute walk and increase the time and duration after several days. How many of us park our cars away from the entrance to a store? One simple change can make a difference.

We all have days when we are not 100 percent. I have whined about going to workout. This occurs when I don't want to workout or run. I wake up and ask myself, "did I really say I was going to exercise this morning?" If I don't get up, I regret it for the rest of the day. After I work out, I'm so glad I did. Those are the days I needed it the most. Even if I don't work out at full effort, I am still doing something good for my body and mind. What are you waiting for to have the body you want?

At my CrossFit box, there are quotes painted on the wall illustrating positive self-talk:

"The Comfort Zone Is a Made Up Place"

"You will never know your limits until you push them"

Where is your comfort zone? How big or small is it? Identify how you live in it. What are you waiting for to move out of it?

A. Three examples of comfort zone

   1. I have never tried this before
   2. I don't want to look stupid trying it
   3. Will I be laughed at?

B. Three ways you can challenge your fitness comfort zone

1. Start by walking a short distance, maybe 10 minutes a day.
2. Ask a friend to exercise with you or ask for help on how to do it.
3. Take a challenge and participate in a fitness event.

You need to be around people that will stretch and challenge you to keep learning – and doing. Push the things that make you uncomfortable.

Another quote from my CrossFit box, "The distance between your dreams and reality is discipline".

What is your **Why**? Why not improve your health? Why wait? If not now, when, and if not you, who? If you put your mind to it, you can do it. It takes discipline.

If you told me 10 years ago, I would finish a triathlon, I would have laughed. I completed the Ramblin' Rose in South Charlotte with a woman who is 75 years old! The goal of Tri It For Life, a training organization, is to get women up and moving! Women of all ages, abilities, and sizes participated in the annual event. Some women learned to swim during training; others hadn't run or biked in decades. All 120 in the Tri It For Life group finished. Now, we're all triathletes! I returned in 2017 as a mentor.

Create your plan for better health. Are you doing it for you or for someone else? Your health is an individual choice.

Do you want to quit smoking? Have you promised yourself or someone else that you would quit?

In 1988, when my brother-in-law had triple by-pass surgery, my sister promised if he recovered from the surgery, she would stop smoking. He recovered, and she continues to smoke today. She wasn't quitting for her.

When my husband and I were having difficulty getting pregnant, I thought by going back to church would help. In looking back, I thought attending church was the only way for the blessing to happen. I was selfish. God had a different plan.

We went through one year of infertility. I started first by taking Clomid to generate eggs. The one side affect was hot flashes! Wow, now I can understand when women tell me they are having their own summer. I have never experienced anything since to that degree!

The next step was my husband giving me hormone shots in my derriere' to stimulate egg growth. I went every morning for a blood test to check my estradiol levels for fertility. The doctor's office called daily to tell us the amount of hormones I should get. Twice in that year, I had intrauterine injections with no luck. We realized we would be unable to have children. My husband was unwilling to adopt; which made me sad. With that in mind, the marriage was the most important relationship.

How does procrastination affect your body, health and mindset?

Are you a serial procrastinator? Are you taking 100 percent responsibility for your health or blaming someone or something else for your procrastination? Action kills procrastination!

Here's how to get things done:

1. Decide you are going to change.
2. Make a priority list (at least three items). One priority should be a challenge outside your comfort zone. Place a *by when* on each health or fitness priority.
3. Get a no nonsense results-oriented accountability partner.
4. Do the work!

What am I waiting *for*?

Your Favorite Things

Give yourself permission to have favorite things.

What are your favorite things? Is it food, sleeping in, reading, cooking, shopping, travel, hunting, driving, volunteering, getting a massage, meditating, dessert, working out, sex, kissing, time with family or friends? Prioritize them.

How often do you enjoy your favorite things?

I love to read. When I give myself permission to read, I am relaxed and present. I am doing something for me!

It can be easy. If it is reading the newspaper, magazine or a book, set a timer. Start at 30 minutes. When the timer goes off, see how you feel. If it feels good, keep going.

What about staying in bed *all* day? I have done this! What a wonderful feeling! I have done it alone and with a significant other. You can have breakfast, lunch and dinner in bed. It's a day to relax, sleep, watch movies, read, and yes, make love.

Indulge! Pamper! Enjoy!

Whatever activity you use to free yourself, enjoy the experience like it's your last day.

What am I waiting *for*?

Team

Do you have a team? What does the word *team* mean to you? Do you have a tribe?

I am part of a woman's group called The Woman's Advantage, an organization to help women develop million-dollar businesses. One of the chapters we covered was about team. I had been away from a corporate position for a couple of years and thought, "I don't have a team." I used to be part of a team in my department.

Having a team as an entrepreneur was foreign to me. I was wrong. I had read the chapter and answered questions in the workbook. When I spoke up at our monthly meeting and said, "I don't have a team," there was silence. The eight women looked at me and said, "We are your team." I quickly learned a team is anyone that supports what you are doing, mentors or coaches or anyone that motivates you is your team. I started thinking about all the people on my team.

Since moving to North Carolina, I have become part of a number of teams: Every Woman Can Be, eWomen, Professional Networking Partners and basketCASE Redefined. My biggest support comes from my business team - Glenn Proctor, Trish Stukbauer, and Sara Dir.

Who is on your team? Who is cheering you on during a graduate or certificate program, when you are training for a sports event, losing weight, working on a hobby or starting a business? Who's got your back? Who can you call day or night?

Find team members that understand and motivate you.

What are you waiting *for*?

EXECUTION

Stay Active and Keep Moving (Own It, Claim It, Share It, Shout It Out)

First, Believe

- Believe in you
- Believe in who you are
- Believe in the contribution you are
- Believe, you matter to yourself
- Believe, you matter to others
- Believe, you are a miracle
- Believe! Believe! Believe!
- I believe_____

Believe is my power word. I wear a bracelet engraved with the word Believe. Every time I feel it or see it, it reminds me to Believe. I am confident. I got this! I deserve and Believe in my success.

Muhammad Ali, one of the greatest boxers of all time, believed in himself and enrolled us in believing it as well.

His famous quote:

"Float like a butterfly, sting like a bee."

This told the world and his opponents what to expect in the ring.

He taunted his opponents with rhythmic sayings and

released an album of spoken work titled, *"I Am the Greatest."*

Here are several other quotes from Muhammad Ali that speak to believing in yourself.

"He who is not courageous enough to take risks will accomplish nothing in life."

I hated every minute of training, but I said, "Don't quit. Suffer now and live the rest of your life as a champion."

We embraced that he was the Greatest and didn't question it. His spoke these words in the 1960s when there was more segregation.

Own it! You have the power over what you do. You must answer to you. We act as if we have to answer to a lot of people. That's because we are afraid of what others think about us. That's our fear factor.

A friend told me about a book - *What You Think Of Me Is None Of My Business* - by Terry Cole-Whittaker that continues to snap me back to reality. We think people are watching us, and they are; some to see how well we do and others to see if we fail. Some are consumed about what they are doing, or not doing, how it looks and if they are doing it right. Sound familiar? I'm not alone.

I typed, "we worry about what others think " in Google and found three quotes that speak to me.

"You wouldn't worry so much about what others think of you if you realized how seldom they do" - Eleanor Roosevelt.

"The greatest prison people live in, is the fear of what other people think" - Anonymous.

"I am in competition with no one. I run my own race, I have no desire to play the game of being better than anyone, in any way shape or form. I just aim to improve to be better than I was before. That's me and I'm free" - Anonymous.

Claim It! Say out loud what you want! Get to the point of yelling it.

Choose your *by when* date. I wanted to write this book and my business partner set a *by when* date. No Excuses!

When you know *What* you *Want, Why* you want it, you *Own it*, you *Claim it,* and *By When* You want it, the *How* will show up.

How often do you talk to yourself about the future? What's next? What's your success plan? What is your self-talk?

Affirmations work.

Louise L. Hay is my favorite author and counselor for affirmations. The following paragraphs were taken from her website.

"An affirmation opens the door. It's a beginning point on the path to change. In essence, you're saying to your subconscious mind: 'I am taking responsibility. I am aware that there is something I can do to change.'"

"When I talk about affirmations, I mean consciously choosing words that will help eliminate something from your life or help create something new."

"Every thought you think and every word you speak is an affirmation. All of our self-talk, our internal dialogue, is a stream of affirmations. You're using affirmations every moment whether you know it or not. You're affirming and creating your life experiences with every word and thought."

"These words are either negative or positive. Yes, we want the positive affirmations. Notice the self-talk you have at different parts of your day. The voice that continues to speak to us even when we think it isn't!"

In coaching and visioning workshops, my business partner and I ask participants to use *one word* to describe themselves. What a challenge for many people! *Resilience* is Glenn's word and mine is *Believe*. For us, these words motivate and generate action. Find *your word* – the one that gets you up in the morning and pushes you throughout the day.

For good things to happen in your life, you must **Claim**

who you are. You may falter or fall back into your "old" self-talk and that is ok as long as you recognize it quickly and get back on your positive journey. This is when you reach out to your accountability partner. Journal, meditate or pray to find the strength that renews your energy. Look in the mirror to find your flow!

I purchased a plaque at the 2016 Carolina Renaissance Festival, an annual event in Huntersville, NC, that reads, "I am Strong! I am Beautiful! I am Powerful! It's all My choice!"

I choose these affirmations as needed for strength or create my own. Here are a few that I created for you:

I am Wonderful! I am Awesome! I am a Wonderful Mom! I am a Wonderful Dad! I am Handsome! I am Healthy! I am Wealthy! I am listened to with love and understanding! I am a Writer! I am Writing a book! (the last two helped me finish this book).

Write three affirmations for yourself.

1. I am _____
2. I am _____
3. I am _____

Be outrageous!

Now that you have claimed who you are, I want you to **Own** it. Wear it like a medal; a broche; a cape; make a t-shirt; it will be a great conversation starter.

Once you create your affirmation, it becomes a part of you. It's in your head. It's in your heart. Feel it with all your senses!

Share it! Shout it Out! This makes it real, it's out there in the universe. Get someone to help you be true to your word and follow through.

Time to get moving. It's the carrot on the stick theory. You are the rabbit chasing it! Create your vision board. Set deadlines. Make a plan.

For me, it's GOPE - goals, obstacles, planning and execution. If we are not achieving our goals, there is something or someone in our way. I'm talking about nots and knots. We all get knotted up because of fear or putting things off.

That's what happened to me. I was asked to create a training program. I was unfamiliar with the material and not sure where to start. I got all knotted up.

We miss a lot of goals because we don't prioritize our time or focus our actions. Yet, we find time for distractions – doing the easy and fun things we want.

One of our biggest obstacles for achieving personal and professional success is the six inches between our ears! To be successful, we must define our mindset, self-talk and level of self-leadership.

When I mentored for the triathlon, I recognized women struggling in their heads. During training for my first triathlon, I had that level of uncertainty.

One mentor said, "you'll do your race like you trained for it." I had to train hard to finish well. In our personal and professional lives, we compete against ourselves first, then we compete against others. Those six inches can take you down or build you up. You may have the negative Nellie/Nate on one shoulder and the positive Patty/Peter on the other shoulder. As long as the positive one is winning, you're winning.

Some of us plan. Others "shoot from the hip." Either way works. I am a planner. I set goals and create steps to achieve positive results. My affirmations and accountability partners help me avoid obstacles, distractions and negative self-talk.

Define your personal journey. Don't be just okay with your direction. Stretch yourself! Create challenging goals!

"If you don't create your own direction, others will help you stay lost." – Glenn Proctor

I knew when I was ready for a challenge. I had just

completed my first 10k. Then the coaches said, "we will train for a half marathon if anyone want to." This is where I had some self-talk. "If not now, when? I ran six miles, what was seven more?"

I ran the half marathon in 2 hours, 13 minutes, and came in 11th out of 33 in my age group 55-59. It wasn't on my bucket list. I didn't have a bucket list at that time. Opportunities like this will come into our lives. Take action!

What is your action? It could be either/or, or both/and.

Here is an example for either/or. You want to work out, but feel you must lose weight before going to the gym. That is either/or. Either you lose weight first and then go to the gym, or not go to the gym because you can't lose the weight. When you are in the either/or mindset, you are deciding it must be one way or the other.

A case for both/and. You can go to the gym and lose the weight at the same time. Don't worry about what you look like. Not everyone is looking at you; they are thinking about their own workout. You made a choice to do something about your health. Find the kind of workout you want, and the kind of gym that will provide what you need.

In the both/and mindset, you are working with choice - a win-win situation. Life is moving downstream with the flow. You are open to ideas and seeing life and health with a different view.

After my divorce, I was taking care of my house - inside and out - including trimming shrubs, trees, pulling weeds and cleaning and maintaining the house.

One day as I pulled into my driveway, I saw a weed sticking out of the stones by the side of the house. I started to cry. I was overwhelmed. After a few minutes, I stopped crying, realizing I am only one person and can only do so much. I like to complete an entire job once I start, but I realized I had to set small goals - work on one area of the yard for two hours. Or, cut three forsythia shrubs rather than all nine. Setting small goals made a difference. I was mentally relieved.

Are you stuck? Don't know where to begin. There is a book called - Eat That Frog *21 Great Ways to Stop Procrastinating and Get More Done in Less Time* by Brian Tracy.

Yuck! And yet, the premise is simple. What is one thing you must do and don't want to? That is the one thing to tackle first. Otherwise, it will weigh on you mentally and physically. Cut the frog into bite size pieces, so it doesn't feel like an elephant in your room!

Are you Awake? Are you Resilient? Are you in Charge of your life? Is your vision Clear? Do you see Opportunity? Are you ready to Plan and Execute? If not, *by when*?

What am I waiting *for*?

I Love You

Three words that mean so much can cause angst, awkwardness, embarrassment, elation or excitement.

Have you waited to tell someone you love them? Concerned they might not feel the same? Or, hoping they would say it first? What is it about saying or hearing, *"I love you"* that produces smiles, fear, euphoria and curiosity? Say it when you *really* feel it. Or, you may miss the opportunity. Love may come when you least expect it or not at all.

Do you love? Are you in love? Two different questions; two different conversations.

I've heard people say, "I told them years ago I love them. They should know." We all need to be reminded how people feel about us and how we feel about those we love. It needs to be said.

I grew up in a household in Corning, a city in upstate New York south of Rochester, with a stay-at-home mom. My dad worked, and I have an older sister and brother. I don't remember any of us saying to each other, "I love you." My mom and dad may have said it behind closed doors.

In March 2014, my sister and I received a call that my mom had fallen at home and it was necessary to fly her by helicopter to a nearby Pennsylvania hospital. Her condition was serious enough to have her on a breathing tube in an intensive care unit. I flew from Charlotte to join my sister in Rochester. We drove down to Corning. On the second day with mom, we realized she was not going to be with us much longer. The hospital chaplain suggested we each say our goodbyes.

My sister went to her bed first, then my brother and then me. When I was leaving and pulling the curtain closed, my dad was standing next to the bed. I heard him say to my mom, "I love you". It was the first time I remember hearing my dad say those words. I thought to myself, there was love between them. I wish they had expressed it more for us to see and hear. At that moment, I felt sad, compassion and empathy. To have been present at that moment was a gift.

Fifty-two years before, I had a similar love feeling. I had broken my right arm at age five and after my cast was taken off, my dad and I were walking down Reynolds Avenue. As he held my hand, I remember him saying, "Squeeze my hand." He had me squeeze his to help me strengthen mine. Even at five, I knew. I felt safe and protected. I knew it was all about me.

I called my dad when I wrote this part of the book and how that small gesture made me feel. He remembered the walk and months earlier when I jumped off the front porch railing and broke my arm. I jumped because I saw my older brother, Michael, jump off the railing onto the driveway. It looked like fun. He told me several times not to jump. I said catch me. He said don't jump. I jumped anyway. He didn't catch me. I was in the hospital in traction for three weeks and then in a cast for a couple months. My dad was amazed at how we remembered those details.

One of the best ways parents and families can bond is to say, *"I love you"* to each other. And, say it in front of the children. We don't know who is listening or watching and what a contribution it may be for them. Kids are always watching and listening.

How do you love? How often do you tell someone, "I love you?" You may think if you say it all the time, it will sound rote and not believable. There are a lot of ways you can tell or show the people in your life you love them. Whisper it, write it on a card, slip a note in a special place, give them a hug or text it. How else can you tell or show them?

There are many people to love in our lives. The most important one is You!

My sister is eight years older. When we were younger and slept in the same room, lying in our beds in the dark, we would play Guess the Object:

"I see something that sees me and it is…"

- as red as red can be or
- as round as round can be or

- as fluffy as fluffy can be or

- as _____

One of us would guess what the object is. It was a lot of fun and we laughed until we fell asleep.

After she graduated high school, my sister moved to Rochester. We would see each other on holidays and special occasions. Through the years, we had hour-long phone conversations to catch up. Our relationship was okay, not real close. Whenever I told her what I was doing in my life, I felt she was being critical of what I chose to do or I wasn't doing it right!

After her husband died in 2012, I spent two weeks with her, helping with the paper work, and primarily being there for emotional support. We got closer.

In recent years, I realized I had a certain way of listening to her. I recognized I was not allowing her to be a contribution to me. In September 2016, I called her with tears in my eyes.

I said, "I love you." Her reply, and I could sense the emotion, "I am here for you and I love you too." I received a card from her the next week, and she wrote, "Thank you for reaching out to my heart."

Who are the people you need to connect with? Write down the names – *right now* - and promise you will contact them by phone or email within the next three days. You can use the blank pages in the back of this chapter.

Back to Self! You are the most important person to love. Look in the mirror, focus on your eyes and say, "I love you". If you can't say it to yourself, how can you say it to others and mean it? If you struggle with self-love, it is time to admit something is holding you back. Journal, meditate, pray or speak to a professional about what it is to love yourself.

Take a Moment:

On a 3x5 card write, I LOVE YOU, and place it on your bathroom mirror. Every time you see the card, look in the mirror and whisper *"I love you"* three times. Fall in love with yourself. Your family, friends and co-workers will notice a change.

One book I highly recommend, *The 5 Love Languages* by Gary D. Chapman. It opened my eyes to my love language and the ways I want to be shown love. It also helps me understand others and what fills their love tank.

I Love You.

What am I *waiting* for?

Mission & Vision

Do you have Mission and Vision statements for your life? I never thought to have either. I do now.

A mission statement is what you tell others how your life is going to be. The vision statement is everything that you envision for your life.

My mission statement: "Live my life to the fullest, experiencing new things every chance possible, continue learning, loving and laughing with friends and family. Die with no songs left."

Vision statement: "Experience all the world has to offer, be present and enjoy each moment."

What am I waiting *for* in creating mission and vision statements for my life?

Bucket List

Do you have a bucket list? It's a list of things you want to accomplish before you die.

Having a bucket list keeps those items alive and is a great reminder of what you want to accomplish. What is on *your* list? Getting a degree, skydiving, painting, writing, travel, changing careers, losing weight, taking a cooking class.

In the past five years, I have done things I never imagined. And, my bucket list continues to grow. It includes taking a cruise, travel to Italy and France, visiting the Norman Rockwell museum in Stockbridge, Massachusetts and remarrying.

As Glenn Proctor, my business partner, says, "as long as you have a bucket and a list, you have a place for your water and your dreams."

What things are you waiting to do? Are you waiting because you think you lack time or money? Are there special things you want to accomplish or places you want to visit? Are these thoughts haunting you year after year and nothing changes? If you don't have a bucket list, make one today!

Take a Minute:

- What are the items on your bucket list?

- What new approach to time can you take?

- What can you do to make more money or change where your money is going?

How serious are you about items on your bucket list?

Think about the movie starring Jack Nicholson and Morgan Freeman.

What am I *waiting* for?

Over Analyzing, Over Thinking

This mental trap is one I continue to work on. It slows decision-making in my personal and professional life. I try to figure things out for myself rather than asking for help. Not wanting to bother someone or thinking they don't have time to talk or to help me. People can say No; they facilitate their own time. People want to be asked and they want to help.

Would you help if someone asked for your help? I am a *Yes* to helping others. Yet, I have to be careful about saying yes. It distracts me from my priorities. When that happens, I need to say, "I can help later or not at all."

Is there something you want right now and are afraid to take action? Or, you think, "I'll never have that." Why can't you have that? Is your analysis your paralysis? Is your life months and years of over thinking and inaction?

What am *I* waiting for?

Making Decisions

How often do we make spur-of-the-moment decisions?

So many of us agonize over making decisions. I am one of those people. Sometimes, I don't think I have all the information I need to make an informed decision. Other times, I know by gut feel and still don't take action. I don't want to make the wrong decision. And, that keeps me in the same place.

This leaves me upset; wishing I had made *a* decision. The best decision is to make a choice even when I don't have all the information. It will never be perfect. Stick by that decision. Making no decision is a decision.

When I continued in the passive/aggressive relationship, that was not a good decision. I didn't follow my gut. I wasn't happy and that was my fault. Deciding to end it opened my energy for a new relationship.

What decision(s) are you waiting to make? Afraid of the outcome or making the wrong decision? Take a risk. In Dale Carnegie's book, *How to Win Friends and Influence People*, think about what is the worst that can happen. It probably won't.

What am *I* waiting for?

Settling?

What is settling? Settling is taking the next best thing that comes along; to get less than what you want. It is thinking you can never find the man or woman of your dreams, have the job you really want, be comfortable financially or acquire certain material things.

I have friends younger than me that say, "I will never find someone." I want to shake them. Too many people I have encountered have a negative mindset, lack of confidence and self esteem. It's all about self-talk. I have older friends that have found love.

Relationship alert! Men and women sharpen your pencils. Be aware of what you really want. What are the deal breakers? What are the must haves?

My deal breakers: smokers, multiple tattoos, beards or heavy drinkers.

Must haves: be faithful, fun, good sense of humor, spontaneous, religious, must love dogs, loves to eat, loves to dance, enjoys art and entertainment, comfortable in jeans and suits, and loves adventure.

If you settle, you will be unhappy. Everything seems wonderful in the beginning; you and they can do nothing wrong. Eventually, you are unhappy and they can do nothing right! You look at them with a critical eye and complain to your friends. Now what?

Are you settling at work and thankful you have a job? Same scenario. You settle for the available job at the time, but you know you can do better. What steps are you taking to improve personally and professionally? Are you settling?

What am *I* waiting for?

Communicating / Communication

This, I believe, is the most difficult <u>thing</u> for people to understand, to do, and to appreciate.

"Communication is the heart of any relationship" - Paula Lesso.

Do you communicate exactly what you want or how you feel? Is your communication clear? Communication is a two-way street. Even a debate has two sides.

Who do you need to communicate with today? Is there something to be said? Was something said and misunderstood? Have there been months or years of miscommunication or no communication? Are you in this situation with family, friends, coworkers, and lovers?

Are you waiting for someone to extend an olive branch or will you take a bold step and reach out?

"Life is short." How many times have we heard that and still not taken action to communicate? I have. It takes a death or serious illness to bring people together and realize how precious life is. Even then, communication is awkward and limited.

Bring me flowers when I am living
Don't bring me them when I am dead,
Let me enjoy them in the giving
My mother always had said.
Let me hold them in my hands
And smell their fragrant scent,
Then I will reminisce of different lands
Before; I am heaven sent.
I will reflect back when I was young
Or, I might think back not long ago,
When I walked underneath the sun
Or, when I felt the wind as it blowed.

Bring me flowers when I am here
Please don't wait until I am gone,
So, I might reflect to a different year
And my memories will last on.
I might reflect to a different time
With every breadth and scent I breath,
And knowing the flowers are mine
Shows how much that you love me.
Let me enjoy the flowers again
Let me feel them on my fingers,
Because I just don't know when;
And how long my memory will linger.

Bring me flowers with a smile
Please don't bring them with any sorrow,
And I will hold them just like a child
As I held you, and held on until tomorrow.

I want to see them once again
As I place them on my table,
And then they will be my friend
And I will greet them while I am able.
They will be a part of me
My mother always had said
So, bring them now to me please
And don't wait until I am dead.

- Randy L. McClave

One of the key strategies of my coaching practice is having my clients communicate what's most important to them. We focus on eliminating barriers and create steps to make our lives better. Like so many clients, I've had to step back, view my life and choose what is most important.

Here's an example: I volunteered as career coach for 30 hours a week. Unfortunately, that much time was detrimental to growing my business. I was the only one that could say no; they weren't going to. After some self-talk, I told the agency I could no longer volunteer. I had to be cognizant of giving my time and experience away.

What is keeping you from communicating? What needs to be said and when?

What am I waiting for?

Determined / Determination

How determined are you to get the best out of life?

Do you believe?
Are you focused?
Have you planned?
Are you executing your plan?

What is the next phase of your life? Are you stuck? I've experienced being stuck; it's a lonely place. The best thing we can do is to seek help. Continue to strengthen our *asking* muscle every day. Are we ready to change our lives?

Ask! Ask! Ask! Remember the Tin Man. Even though he was strong and brave, he needed help. If he hadn't asked for help, even in his weak voice, he would still be stuck.

When I get that feeling, I challenge myself with positive self-talk. And, ask for help. Every time I step into my CrossFit box, facilitate a workshop, give a speech or have a coaching session, I am determined to be successful.

How can you be more determined in your life?

When you are determined, nothing gets in your way.

What am I waiting for?

What Are You Waiting For?

That is the question.

There are so many things in life that we wait for. We can achieve personal and professional success when we take action. Without action, nothing happens. A lot of talk is just a lot of talk. I remind myself that God honors action.

As I mentioned throughout this book, there have been times in my life where I waited to make crucial decisions. Now I live by this motto: "If I don't take action today, the day will pass and the decision is still to be made."

You have been called to action. What do you want to change in your life? Make a list. Ask yourself, "What Am I Waiting For?" What is in the way? How can you transform your mindset to make better choices?

I asked, "What Am I Waiting For?" at the end of every section as a way for you to think about making changes. It's your personal call to action.

If you have a grain of sand in your shoe, you have to get rid of it. This reminds me of a tale:

There are two men sitting in their rockers on a porch with a hound dog laying between them. Periodically, the hound dog raises its head to howl and lay it back down. After several times, the one man asks, "why does the dog do that?" The owner says, "the dog is laying on a nail and it isn't irritating enough for him to move."

How long do we let something irritate us before we do something about it? If we continue to let situations or shortcomings bother us, we will be uncomfortable. We either choose to be uncomfortable or we take steps to change.

In the beginning of the book, I asked that you say the following statements out loud. Say them out loud again and see if a different one stands out for you.

What am I waiting for?
What **Am** I waiting for?
What am **I** waiting for?
What am I **Waiting** for?
What am I waiting **For**?

Notice which question stood out for you this time. Compare your answers. Is it the same question or different? How do you feel right now?

Before I say thank you for reading this book, I ask again:

What Are You Waiting For?

Today is the best day to start "living".

Thank You.
For coaching information or interviews and book reviews, contact Paula Lesso at www.paulalesso.com.

CPSIA information can be obtained
at www.ICGtesting.com
Printed in the USA
FSHW020004040121
77369FS